GAMES NIGHT

ALSO BY ANDY JACKSON

Poetry

The Assassination Museum (Red Squirrel Press, 2010)
A Beginner's Guide to Cheating (Red Squirrel Press, 2015)
The Saints Are Coming (Blue Diode Publishing, 2020)

As Editor

Split Screen (Red Squirrel Press, 2012)
Tour de Vers (Red Squirrel Press, 2013)
Double Bill (Red Squirrel Press, 2014)
Seagate III (Discovery Press, 2016)
Perthshire 101 (Tippermuir Books, 2022)

As Co-Editor

With W. N. Herbert

Whaleback City (Dundee University Press, 2013)
New Boots and Pantisocracies (Smokestack Press, 2016)

With Brian Johnstone

Scotia Extremis (Luath Press, 2019)

With George Szirtes

The Call of the Clerihew (Smokestack Press, 2019)
More Bloody Clerihews (Smokestack Press, 2022)

Games Night

Andy Jackson

RED SQUIRREL PRESS

First published in 2023 by Red Squirrel Press
36 Elphinstone Crescent
Biggar
South Lanarkshire
ML12 6GU
www.redsquirrelpress.com

Edited by Elizabeth Rimmer

Cover image: © Leila Alekto Photo / shutterstock.com

Layout, design and typesetting by Gerry Cambridge
gerry.cambridge@btinternet.com

Copyright © Andy Jackson 2023

Andy Jackson has asserted his right to be identified as the author of this work in accordance with Section 77 of the Copyright, Designs and Patents Act 1988.
All rights reserved.

A CIP catalogue record for this book is available from the British Library.

ISBN: 978 1 913632 46 5

Red Squirrel Press is committed to a sustainable future.
This publication is printed in the UK by Imprint Digital using Forest Stewardship Council certificated paper.
www.digital.imprint.com

Contents

Games Night

Snap · 11
Escape from Colditz · 12
Musical Chairs · 13
Monopoly · 14
Hangman · 15
Rock, Paper, Scissors · 18
Chess · 19
Risk · 21
Jenga · 22
Mousetrap · 23
Dominoes · 24
Trivial Pursuit · 25

Place Games

City of Nine Trades · 29
A Very British Rendition · 32
From the Sewers · 34
Regime Change · 35
Knackery · 36
Swan Upping · 37
My Father Teaches Bears to Whistle The Red Flag · 38
The Ghost Olympiad · 39
How I Made It Big in America · 40
What's Made Milngavie Famous · 41
Gongoozlers · 43
Murrayfield · 44
Talos over Tayside · 45
James Tytler (1745–1804) · 46
Billy Bytheway · 47
Scaffies · 48
Caledonia · 50

Word Games

Your 12-point Plan for Poetry Success · 55
Brompton Cocktails · 57
Rollback · 58
Tiny Clanger Triolet · 60
Galaxy · 61
I Found This at My Ear · 62
If You Are Not as Tall as Me You Cannot Ride This Ride · 63
…Who Loved This Place · 64
Just Need to Check You're Not a Robot · 65
Dementia Song · 66
Treppenwitz · 68
Everyman's Encyclopaedia, 1972 · 70
Two Poems for the Undecided · 73
On Being Mistaken for Another Poet · 74
Succession Planning · 75
Enquiry Desk, Scottish Poetry Library · 76

Acknowledgements · 79
A NOTE ON THE TYPES · 80

For my wife, who hates board games.

Games Night

A Compendium of 12 Poems for All the Family

Snap

A game of 2–8 players of any age

Games	Life	I	Having
Of	Is	Tried	Acute
Pure	Mostly	Memorising	Hearing
Chance	Chance;		
	SNAP!		
		The	Has
Negate	Luck	Order	Many
The	Is	Of	Advantages;
Advantages			
SNAP!			
	Not	The	All
Of	On	Cards;	Cards
			SNAP!
Practice;	The	The	
		SNAP!	
			Sound
Being	Same	Cards	Slightly
Lucky	Axis	Conspired	Different
Is	Of	To	In
The	Variables	Become	The
Only	As	Unmemorable.	Hand.
Skill.	Skill.		
	SNAP!		

Escape From Colditz

For 3–6 Players Aged 12+

He sank his seventh lager, told me what
the game had learned him about life
in those adolescent nights, sustained
by cold pizza and Rush albums through
to small hours, flatmates consummating
noisy lust on the other side of the wall.

He said he discovered it's easier to bribe
a guard than bluff it out; that hanging
round the chapel gets you nowhere;
that the staff car can only take you so far;
that not having a strategy is a strategy;
that the bad guys always had more fun.

He hadn't played the game in years. He'd
never been to Germany; had no wish to.
I told him how by twenty I'd assembled
my escape kit, cashed in my *Do Or Die*.
He left without a smile or word, playing
his *Shoot To Kill* card all the way home.

Musical Chairs

For any number of players, of any age

Each time the music stops another person loses their place.
Stop the music. Time another person loses their place.
Another person stops, loses the time, place, music.
Music stops another person losing the place.
Stop the music. Another person, place.
Another place. The music stops.
Music! The place stops.
Stop the music.
Music stops.
Stop.

Monopoly

For 2–6 players aged 8+

Take me round those streets again,
from purple plush to brownfield site,
to the stations of cross commuters
where the multitude of honest losers
make just enough to keep the lights
lit and make it to another month-end.

The banker has called in our loans
and all the houses that we mortgaged
to the chin have been repossessed.
Winter, and the Community Chest
is so much firewood. It's a bull market,
and we all have rings in our noses.

We've played too long; now all we see
in faces are buyers, sellers and debtors.
The £10 prize I won in a beauty contest
goes into the kitty for a place up west
among the *arrivistes*, where bank errors
are all in our favour and parking is free.

I met a top-hatted man from Park Lane
and don't apply to us for credit my friend,
as we find a smack in the teeth often offends.
I pack my things, return to the board,
tell myself again that this is only a game.

Hangman

A word game for two players of any age

```
_ _ _ _ _ ' _   _ _ _   _ _ _ _ _ _ _   _ _ _ _ _
_ _ _ _ ' _   _ _ _   _ _ _ _ _ _ _   _ _ _ _ _
```

E
```
_ E _ _ _ ' _   _ _ E   _ _ _ _ _ _ _   _ _ _ _ E
_ _ _ E ' _   _ _ E   _ _ _ _ _ _ _   _ _ _ _ E
```

T
```
_ E _ T _ ' _   T _ E   _ _ _ T _ _ _   _ _ _ _ E
_ _ _ E ' _   T _ E   _ _ T T _ _ _   _ _ _ _ E
```

P
```
_ E _ T _ ' _   T _ E   _ _ _ T _ _ _   _ _ _ _ E
_ _ _ E ' _   T _ E   _ _ T T _ _ _   _ _ _ _ E
```

F
```
_ E _ T _ ' _   T _ E   _ _ _ T _ _ _   _ _ _ _ E
_ _ _ E ' _   T _ E   _ _ T T _ _ _   _ _ _ _ E
```

N
```
_ E _ T _ ' _   T _ E   _ _ _ T _ N _   N _ _ _ E
_ _ _ E ' _   T _ E   _ _ T T _ N _   _ _ _ _ E
```

Y
```
_ E _ T _ ' _   T _ E   _ _ _ T _ N _   N _ _ _ E
_ _ _ E ' _   T _ E   _ _ T T _ N _   _ _ _ _ E
```

O
```
_ E _ T _ ' _   T _ E   _ _ _ T _ N _   N O O _ E
_ O _ E ' _   T _ E   _ _ T T _ N _   _ O O _ E
```

R

_E_T_'_ T_E ___T_N_ NOO_E
_O_E'_ T_E __TT_N_ _OO_E

S

_E_T_'S T_E ___T_N_ NOOSE
_O_E'S T_E __TT_N_ _OOSE

B

_E_T_'S T_E ___T_N_ NOOSE
_O_E'S T_E __TT_N_ _OOSE

W

_E_T_'S T_E W__T_N_ NOOSE
_O_E'S T_E __TT_N_ _OOSE

X

_E_T_'S T_E W__T_N_ NOOSE
_O_E'S T_E __TT_N_ _OOSE

I

_E_T_'S T_E W_ITIN_ NOOSE
_O_E'S T_E __TTIN_ _OOSE

Z

_E_T_'S T_E W_ITIN_ NOOSE
_O_E'S T_E __TTIN_ _OOSE

H

_E_TH'S THE W_ITIN_ NOOSE
_O_E'S THE __TTIN_ _OOSE

A

EATH'S THE WAITIN NOOSE
_O_E'S THE __TTIN_ _OOSE

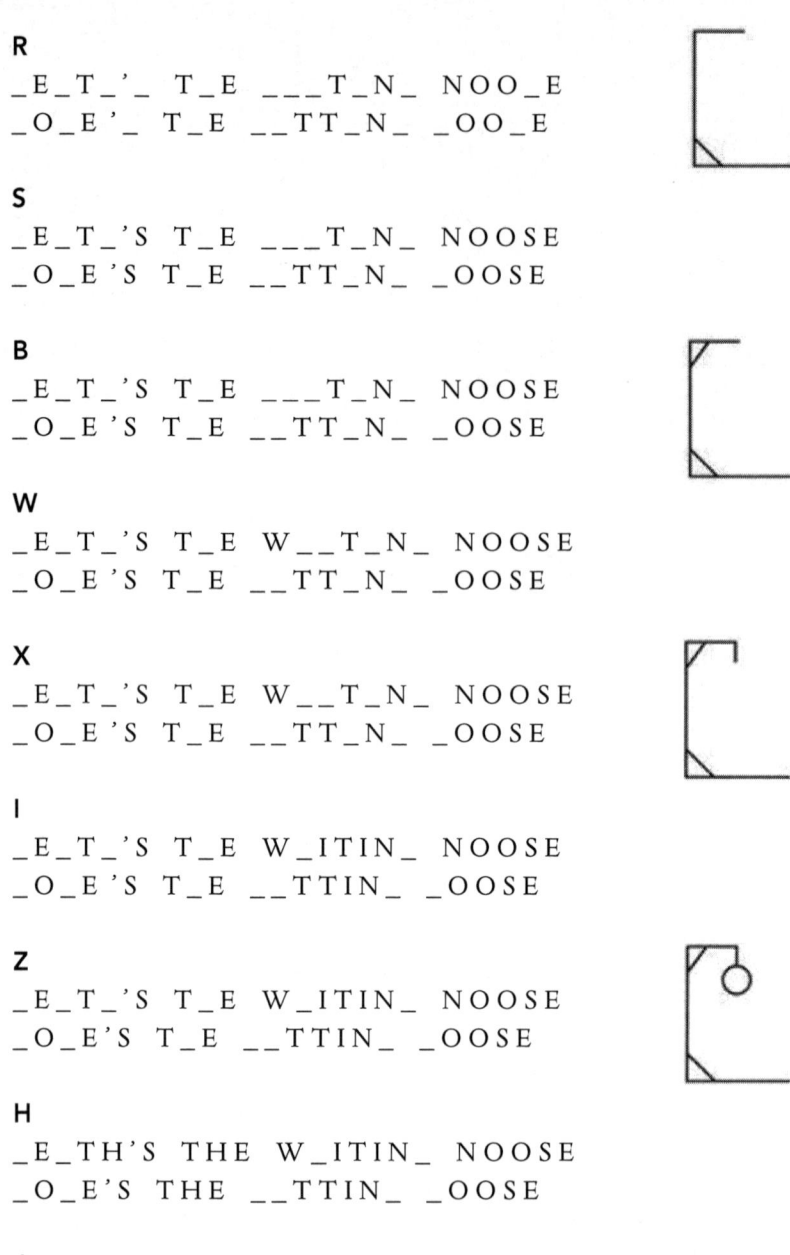

L
EATH'S THE WAITIN NOOSE
LO_E'S THE __TTIN_ LOOSE

C
EATH'S THE WAITIN NOOSE
LO_E'S THE C_TTIN_ LOOSE

Rock, Paper, Scissors

A game for two people of any age

Paper wraps rock.
Rock blunts scissors.
Scissors cut paper.
Paper hoards ink.
Ink writes word.
Word lights darkness.
Darkness eats courage.
Courage talks jeopardy.
Jeopardy seasons routine.
Routine lulls frailty.
Frailty orbits broken.
Broken wants glue.
Glue binds pieces.
Pieces seek whole.
Whole tells story.
Story conceals ending.
Ending closes book.
Book freezes moment.
Moment defines eternity.
Eternity permits folly.
Folly paints past.
Past shouts warning.
Warning wears veil.
Veil masks doubt.
Doubt denies wisdom.
Wisdom bears scorn.
Scorn leaves scars.
Scars forge steel.
Steel makes scissors.
Scissors cut paper.
Paper wraps rock.

Chess

A game for two players of any age

> —For Tom Dickson

e4 e6	White with her trusty Sophic opening.
d3 d5	Passive aggression?
Nd2 Nf6	Black opens with his customary Mancunian defence.
g3 c5	Risky, but opens up a promising new line of expression.
Bg2 Nc6	Swift pawn exchange.
Ngf3 Be7	Black keeping parity, but it's tense.
O-O O-O	White not moving with urgency yet,
e5 Nd7	Which might be ominous?
Re1 b5	White develops an opening,
Nf1 b4	Though no easy route to Mate.
h4 a5	Black still seems unaware of the approaching menace.
Bf4 a4	Black sees it now, but it's several moves too late.
a3 bxa3	The power has shifted.
bxa3 Na5	White posing all the questions.
Ne3 Ba6	Was this Black's crucial mistake?
Bh3 d4	Black losing his cool.
Nf1 Nb6	Attempts a sacrifice to disguise his true intentions.
Ng5 Nd5	White sees through it.
Bd2 Bxg5	White clinical to the point of cruel.
Bxg5 Qd7	Into the endgame.
Qh5 Rfc8	Does Black see a chink of light?
Nd2 Nc3	All or nothing now for Black.
Bf6 Qe8	Nothing the more likely.
Ne4 g6	Black's fate now all but sealed.
Qg5 Nxe4	Queen calls up her knight.
Rxe4 c4	Breathtaking.
h5 cxd3	Leaves Black's assets spread too widely.

Rh4 Ra7	White in total control.	
Bg2 dxc2	King's Gambit declined.	
Qh6 Qf8	Black fatally exposed and out of moves.	
Qxh7+	Black resigns.	

Move sequence is taken from a game between Bobby Fischer vs Lhamsuren Myagmarsuren in 1967, containing what has been described as 'the greatest quiet move of all time' (Bg2 at Move 29).

Risk

For 2-6 players aged 10+

    —After Nick Middleton's An Atlas of Countries That Don't Exist

Yakutsk from Kamchatka with ten armies
Siberia from Yakutsk with eight armies
Ural from Siberia with six armies
Ukraine from Ural with five armies
Scandinavia from Ukraine with three armies
Iceland from Scandinavia with two armies
United Kingdom from Iceland with one army
Doggerland from the United Kingdom with one army
Ruritania from Doggerland with one army and an old atlas
Ruthenia from Ruritania with one army with one voice for one day
Catalonia from Ruthenia with no armies but a consultation of citizens
Christiania from Catalonia with a stoned army and a herbal economy
Transnistria from Christiania with no armies but the echo of a purge
Ogoniland from Transnistria with a private army paid in petroleum
Lakotah from Ogoniland with nothing but the fragments of a song
Tibet from Lakotah with a thousand smiling monks in snowfall
Antarctica from Tibet with only what you can carry in your pocket
Elgaland-Vargaland from Antarctica with a dream of a forged passport

Jenga

For 2 or more players aged 6+

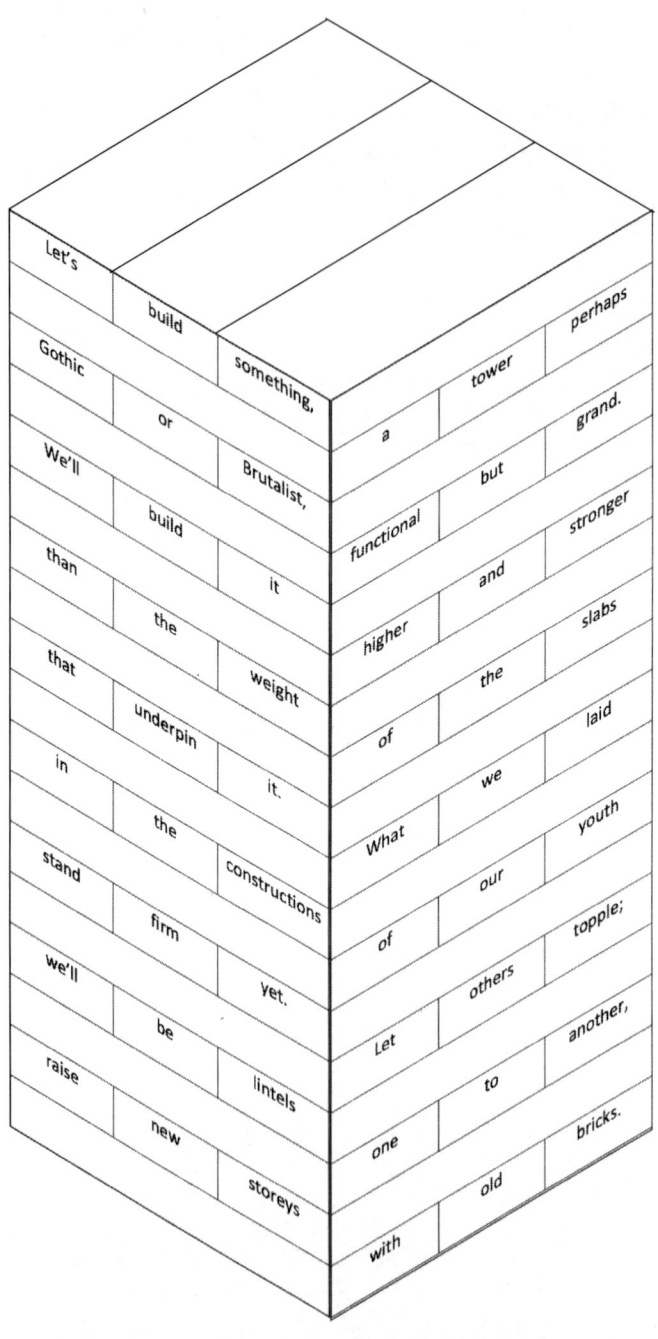

Mousetrap

A game for 2–4 players aged 6 and above

Turn the crank, set the gears in motion,
lever slaps the stop sign to the boot
that kicks the bucket, tips the marble down
the broken staircase, down the chute
to push the rod to drop another marble
through the bath on to the diving board
that springs the diver headlong to the tub
that shakes the pole that holds the cage
that ric-racs down to trap the mouse.

The mouse untraps itself, casts its cage
into the air to still the tub that spits
the diver to his stand and hurls the ball
up through the roof to root the rod
and send the marble sliding up the gutter
to the foot of the stairs that climb up to
the bucket which has filled itself again
and kicks a heel against a clanking piston,
crashes the gears and cranks the turning arm.

The stairs unstep the pinball to the boot
that climbs the leaking roof that fills
the bucket from the bath and kicks
the diver down the culvert to the spring
that heels the hand onto the gears
that breaks the foot and frees the root
and ratchets down the rod into the tub
to stop the stand that turns the hand
into the cage that falls to mouse the trap.

Dominoes

For 2–4 players of any age

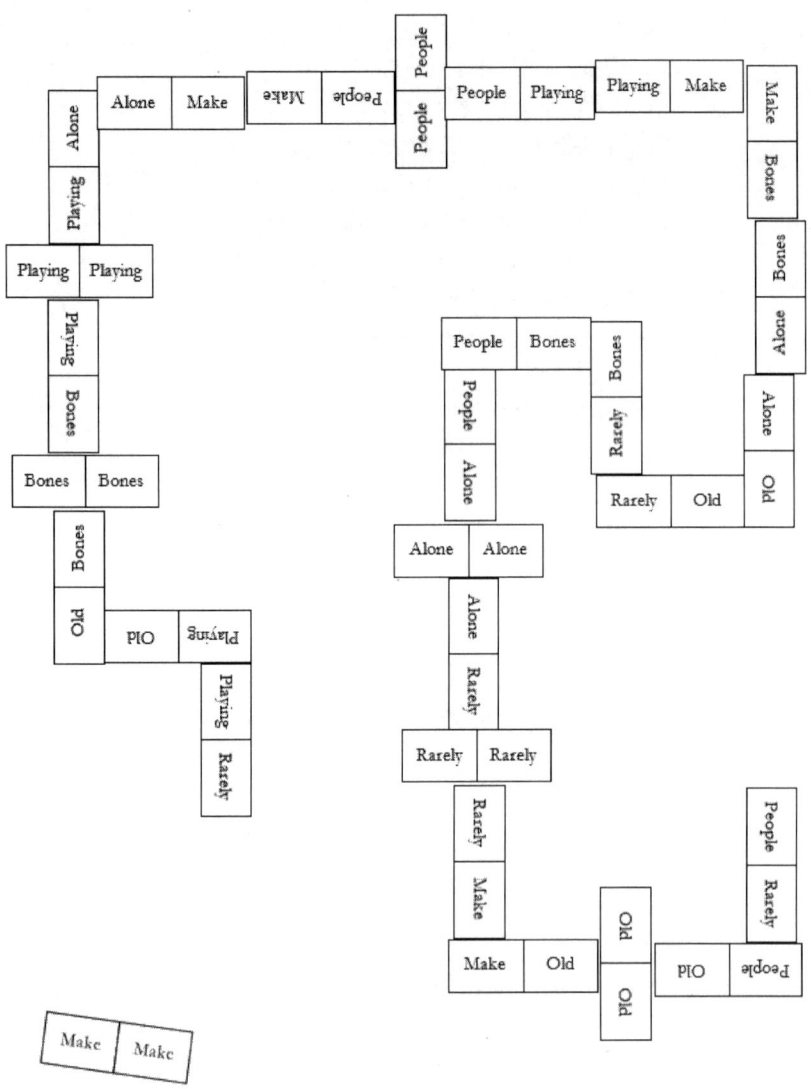

Trivial Pursuit

A game for 2-6 players aged 16 and above

- (G) Which religious festival is also the name of an island in the Pacific?
- (E) Which superhero is weakened by exposure to Kryptonite?
- (H) Which Saint's Day is celebrated on the 26th of December?
- (AL) Which British novelist wrote 'Mansfield Park'?
- (SN) What kind of creature is a Chow-Chow?
- (SL) In which parlour game are contestants only allowed to mime?

- (G) No pursuit is trivial; all knowledge is specific.
- (E) Each fact is waiting to step forward into the light.
- (H) Intelligence is more than the ability to remember.
- (AL) The answer is the answer. There are no half-marks.
- (SN) Cognitive freefall: your phone can't help you now.
- (SL) I'll have to hurry you. Sorry, you're out of time.

[25]

Place Games

City of Nine Trades

> *Dundee's 'Nine Incorporated Trades' were formed in the 16th Century. They were: Bakers, Cordiners, Glovers, Tailors, Bonnetmakers, Fleshers, Hammermen, Weavers and Dyers.*

Of the Solemn Order of
Biochemists, absorbed in
their buildings, bright-lit through
the mislaid hours, touring
the less fashionable suburbs
of the genome, grooming
lymphocytes for
their moment of action;

Of the Estimable League of
Jetwash Operators,
the drookit undead, blaw-ins
from Albania and Kurdistan,
scouring at the dods
of mud till they can see
their gaunt faces
looming in the bonnet;

Of the Worshipful Company
of Journalists, agents of
the Fourth and Fifth Estate,
artisans of slant and
skew and angle,
selling influence wholesale,
looking for the story
in the story;

Of the Venerable Lodge
of Gamesmiths, pixels
jangling in their pockets
as they level up, work

on special moves,
their DNA woven
through a billion lines of code,
yet elusive as vapourware;

Of the Loyal Guild of
Museum Curators, stewards
of artefact and canvas, busy
in their galleries and cliff-toothed
pyramids, but also those
who catalogue the streets,
husbanders of haver,
cant and scuttlebutt;

Of the August Union of
Football Supporters,
facing off on Tannadice Street
like the Spoiling of the Dyke,
sharing the air of the city, yet
dead to each other one day
out of seven, and oh, oh, oh,
who's the bastard in the black?;

Of the Reputable Coalition
of Smartphone Repairers,
guided by these principles:
1) Every cracked screen
is unique as a snowflake,
2) Some things are not
meant to be unlocked, and
3) Life is Pay As You Go;

Of the Virtuous Craft
of Poets, Makars of light,
alchemists, reverse engineers
and holders-up of mirrors,
polishing the unlovely,

tarnishing the pure,
and always one edit
short of perfection;

And of the Noble and Ignoble
Tradeless, masters of the things
we have not learned
to value, treading
the skitie road between
indolence and industry,
schooled not by University
but by the universe.

A Very British Rendition

> *'[The Bill of Rights] will stop terrorists and other serious foreign criminals who pose a threat to our society from using spurious human rights arguments to prevent deportation.'*
> (Conservative Party Manifesto 2015)

This is no Caribbean getaway. Planes
that land here do not flicker up the list
on some arrivals board, nor do trains
roll in at night, panting in the mist
as furtive cargoes disembark. The lags
we drag in here don't get to choose
their clothes; no ankles go untagged.
We have no days, no names, no news.

The compound is secure; our dogs
patrol the fence, and in the basement
we're examining the content of your blogs.
Here we have an unredacted statement
where the grip on rights you think
you hold is slackened off by stealth
—don't you keep up with the news? Blink,
and they're rescinded. Like yourself.

We've muted the birdsong, pixellated
any views of note, watered down
the water. We bodyswerve outdated
practices—as servants of the crown
we're pledged to quality control,
and have introduced a strict embargo
on the cruder methods—gone the cold
thrill of waterboard or bastinado
beat; these days we prefer the long-lens
photos of your wife and kids, or rooms
of purest white to bleach the sense

of what you are, or were. *With whom
were you affiliated? Who recruited
you? Which articles do you invoke?*
Round here we keep it simple, stupid,
and everyone but you is in on the joke.

From the Sewers

I swear I saw one in the pipes,
draped with condoms, bacon rind,
chomping plump rats and roaches,
diving at the flicking-on of torches,
sculling down the godforsaken rivers
of this city in its unforgiving winter.

Neighbour says she saw a creature take
a brace of mallards in the boating lake,
watch a dead log become a hulk
of muscled bark, raise a storm of blood
and broken reeds, heard the quiet
of the water settle back into the night.

They say that someone flushed it down
a pan, thinking it would surely drown
or die of hunger, but like a refugee
it must have found a way to breathe,
to swim, toughen up and take its place,
at the head of the chain, find a mate.

They are surely reproducing now, birthing
babies in the darkness, nursing
them to potency and lairs of their own,
swarming where they once swam alone.
Maybe they can smell the stink of fear
above ground. Maybe they're already here.

Regime Change

I'm here to sweep the empty smiles away,
reclaim the unequivocal reply. The books
from which we sprang have been revised,
the songs we sang together are now off
the playlist. Acts of faith have been repealed.

I represent the things you want but cannot say,
even the unsayable. Papers have no truck
with radicals whose dreams cannot be realised,
and though I can't pretend it won't be tough,
it's not through compromise that we are healed.

You recall those all-night sittings? We grew old
before our time, saw our love phased out
within five years. I know that you were swayed
by other parties, dandled by their spin at night
and, unavoidably, this house divided.

They said I was finished, left out in the cold
for good this time, but even in the drought
between affairs I watched while laws were made
and broken. But look; I'm still black and white,
and red all over. The people have decided.

Knackery

The beast is lowing at the abattoir door, plump
and ready for the stun-gun, the stagger, slump,
the slug behind the ear. Hooves are lopped, stumps
shorn of meat, ribs cracked open. A Latino with a pump
sucks up the entrails of America, glistening in the sump.
All is rendered to an acceptable carcass, fit to be dumped
while in the tower, waiters serve prime cuts. Diners thump
the tables, call for sweetbreads, offal, the head, the rump.

Swan Upping

Young men in scarlet take to varnished skiffs
to scull through rushes, scour the muddied creeks
for cygnets straggling in the upstream drift,
to capture, itemise, ring and release.
We watch the ancient census from the bank,
the pageantry of time, the freakish laws,
yet all the colours can't disguise the black
and white of how it is and always was.

Once a year we count our own possessions,
each to each, both the objects and the space
between them; a husbandry, protection
for the delicate ecology of days.
Number them if you must—the swans, the stars.
Count what can be counted; the rest are ours.

My Father Teaches Bears to Whistle The Red Flag

—for Catia Montagna

Morning waves away the moon,
and father's striding out again.
His footsteps light among the pines,
he whistles for the benefit
of bears who startle easily,
a warning he is coming by.

He hears the sound of snuffling,
then through the brindled light it comes:
a lonely yowl, distinct and gruff,
above the sounds of foraging,
reclusive bear soliloquy,
essayed on a single note.

Another day, another stroll,
the same tune whistled once again,
the furtive Bear sends back two notes.
Primavera then *estate,*
each day holds another note
as beast is tamed by melody.

By *autunno* forest rings
to joyful Bear's diapason,
and other creatures find a voice,
for there is always more to sing.
My father doesn't whistle now
and it is Bear that calls the tune:

Inverno comes: fast falls the sun.
The songs we learned are nearly done.
So raise the ursine standard high,
beneath these trees we'll live and die.
Though marmots flinch and jackals sneer,
we'll keep the red flag flying here.

The Ghost Olympiad

Revenants gather at the stadium
to random-test the Tug-of-War team, drugs
and animus. In the gymnasium
spectral men are climbing ropes, swinging clubs.
There's underwater swimming in the pool,
ordeal by breath, by any other name.

We try to understand: there must be rules,
but not ones we can follow at these games.
The arts that we have learned and somehow lost—
standing jumps, pentathlon of the muses—
once were Olympian and bore the cost
of thick sweat and lonely hours and bruises.
These too will fade: all we can do is grieve,
dig our mortal heels in, take the strain, *heave.*

Tug-of-War last featured at the 1920 Olympics in Antwerp.

How I Made It Big in America

I stopped listening to the news and started reading entrails.

I only ate at breakfast: champagne and grits.

I took the freight elevator and the fire escape; they never saw me coming.

I learned there were only six basic faces (though infinite variations),
and that each once belonged to a sailor.

I workshopped my prejudices and launched them as a range of products.

I rebranded each time the IPR lawyers tracked me down.

I learned the Fifth Amendment is duplicity with good PR.

I rejected the American Dream in favour of the American Action Plan.

I developed a work ethic; *just glad to be here* is nowhere near.

I held certain truths to be self-evident, but that everything else was fair game.

I abandoned life when I discovered it was scouting my successor.

I abandoned liberty when I found it had no perfect rhymes.

I abandoned the pursuit of happiness when it stopped in its tracks, turned and went for me.

I never stopped looking for loopholes.

What's Made Milngavie Famous

—'The more that you learn, the more places you'll go' (Dr Seuss)

How did you find us here? I say I entered
Hyperborea into the TomTom, drove north

until the placid harpy of the dashboard
said *you have reached your destination*.

He takes my paw in his, feels for tremors,
an impostor's twitch. *Where do you stay?*

I answer *Here and there*. He says *But sir,
no man can live in two places at once.*

We stand before his crinkled map,
a melting face in profile, borders drawn,

redrawn. His blacksmith's thumb,
bruised nail where the hammer overshot,

traces out the southwest passage,
hovers over atolls of village and burgh.

His fingers sweep across the silent chart
to jab on a pinprick town. *Say the name.*

Here comes the only test that matters:
already I have one foot in the snare.

Strathaven. Findochty. Kirkcudbright.
Garioch. Kilconquhar. Athelstaneford.

Now I'm in the sightline of a cocked rifle
—*who goes there?*—but I have shibboleths

of my own, perfected at my father's knee,
codes wrought in the forge of antiquity:

Daubhill. Slaithwaite. Gateacre.
Quernmore. Rawcliffe. Wavertree. Blackley.

See how language uses us for sport,
laughing as we feebly try to reconnect,

permitting us to live both here and there,
speaking names that echo back correct.

Gongoozlers

They watched you climb the six-flight stair,
displaying your infallible technique,
striding down the towpath like the Prince
of the Riser, busy with your business.
You must be used to this; everywhere
the watchers working up critiques,
all hydrologists or privateers, convinced
the sea is in their bones, their mistress.

Marshalled in the basin of their lives,
so many of them drift like empty boats,
sometimes skippered by their surly wives,
but mostly happy just to be afloat.
They handle like a vessel with no draught,
barges towed behind a fleet of smarter craft.

Murrayfield

Flowers are in bloom again, masses flowing
past the orphaned clock, through the gates
and up the stairs, dripping February rain.
I came here for the noble drama of the war,
the lightning two-act play, the ceilidh birl
and set, part majesty, part butchery.
Here is the taut ensemble down below,
still giants, even from the highest gallery;
the pudding-headed pachyderms, all gum
and solid sinew; the sugar-crusted feet
and spotless kit of supple ballerinos
wary of the touchline and its precipice;
the gimlet-eyed professor, surfacing from
rucks of flesh with his hunk of meat—
the bladder/ball—the perfect plot device.

Down at stageside you can hear the snarl
and champing of the two front rows,
see the nostrils purged of steam and snot,
smell the black arts in the unlit mine
of the scrum. Then the ball comes loose, alive
and dancing through a dozen pairs of hands,
unshackled from the script to improvise its end.
Up here in the roaring stand it all plays out
in high-def; the pauses while the pails of blood
are emptied, passages of *pas de basque*
and *Grand Guignol*. The chief protagonist
emerges from the wings, fists like gnarls,
waiting for his chance to influence the plot
praying life will, just for once, offload
a good clean ball, open up a clear run to the line.

Talos Over Tayside

This city harbours many minor Titans,
built into the buttresses of tenements,
cast in bronze, or poured like concrete
into bridge supports, or under car parks.

I am one of them; mythic yet enlightened,
elusive, though familiar as elements
of brick and burn. I know the streets,
the local dialect, though I keep it dark

in case my accent gives the game away.
By night I watch the sons of whalers,
weavers, berry-pickers, making their sport
among the nightclubs and the gin mills

of the city, like some mummer's play.
I've many names; you can call me Talos,
creaking giant, scourge of Argonauts,
forged by superstition in the Cretan hills.

That life is gone, but this one is mine;
I'll climb down from my plinth, stand taller
than the Law, then wade into the river
to my knees, gannets wheeling in my wake.

I will eat this city, one postcode at a time,
then lift a three-headed rig from the water,
shake its crew like salt across the Sidlaws,
and use it as a toothpick. Let the earth quake

as I dance, houses crumbling into snow
until there's not a single building left alive.
When the smog of dust clears you will know
that what a place is truly made of will survive.

James Tytler (1745–1804)

I saw the pantheon of aeronauts: you were not there.
No anthem of the skies extolled your name, no fanfare
over Calton Hill or Angus Glens, just the rolling haar
of time, your glory cowled in the cloth of nightmare.

I found the pantheon of prophets; there you were,
still breathing your dreams of enterprise like hot air
into a frail balloon, no more than silk and angelhair
which, if it could carry us, could take us anywhere.

Billy Bytheway

It caught ye aince again; that same dwam—
just eight, doon Mornin Noon & Nicht
fir messages—ten-pack o Lambert & Butler—
bare-scud save yir sister's baffies,
naebdy sayin naethin; aa lookin away.

Yon's yir faither wi his heavy an his dram
at thi bar like a coo hingin ower a dyke,
haufway atween thi howff an thi gutter,
a ghaist amang thi schemies an thi scaffies,
abdy swallyin thir ain gless o waes.

An ye, wha life nudges alang like a laum
tae thi skemmels, blint by the licht,
smearin oan the lippy like it's butter,
tryin oan yir mither's voice, thi way she laughs
at aa thi stupit hings yir faither says,

ye huvna realised thi time has cam
tae step oot thi museum o yir mind an ficht
fir whit yir chyngin intae. Open up thi shutters,
cut thi labels fae the dress an jist be happy
that yir aywis wha ye are in yir ain claes.

Scaffies

No bins emptied today; just a row
of them in sober accord at the roadside,

and the village Facebook page aglow
with ferment. Eleven o'clock, no sign

or sound of the low-revving lorry
emptying away the week past

so we can start again. I worry
something important in the post

may have been torn up and thrown out
with the weekend papers, unread

for the most part. The drought
of an *unprecedented* summer has bred

flies of all species, fat, agitated,
persistent yet aimless, a visitation

around the overflowing bins. Frustrated,
I cycle through the sombre stations

on the TV but there's only the same
view from different camera angles,

like a bad screensaver. I look out again
across to number 96—a lit candle

in the lounge window. At half past two.
A growl of gears from up the street—

maybe the scaffies coming at last? No,
just the beetling man to read the meter.

I've separated the things that should stay
from the packages they come in but still

I cannot throw the packaging away.
They'll come again next week, or never will.

Caledonia

> *'Caldonia! Caldonia! What makes your big head so hard?'*
> *(Louis Jordan and the Tympany Five)*

I don't know if you can see
my name on the label Mum had sewn
into my shirts. It's there for me,
my friend, so when I am alone

I can take a keek under my collar,
mind the man I used to be before
I pitched up in these parts, smaller,
dumber than the sum of the wars

we fought with you. Back then I
was lean and lanky, great big feet,
ignorant of how the land and sky
could be unfolded like a sheet

before me and beyond, waking
sooner every day to forest choirs
and corbie calls, the shaking
of the land by sea, persistent fires

long put out in places I had drifted
from. Mama said 'Son, keep away
from there, its grudges and its frigid
people, lousy with laments, the day

long gone when anyone might ask
them what they know or think'
but all she saw were English masks,
the jokes recalled in midst of drink,

the history that wasn't hers. I've been
telling new stories, singing songs
I do not own, watching submarines
put to sea, their payloads long

unwanted. I see how the nation breaks
and blends and bonds. I'm scarred
for life, but maybe that is what it takes,
what it is that makes our big heads hard.

Word Games

Your 12-Point Plan for Poetry Success

Adapted from Stephan Iscoe's '12-Point Plan for Personal Success' and the 'South Lakeland District Council Display Screen Equipment Workstation Setup 12-Point Plan'

1. Adjust your seat height so that elbows are approximately level with the desk edge. Your imagination should be in a relaxed, neutral position. It will be asking questions of you, so pay attention.

2. Start by smiling back at your reflection in the nearest mirror. If you do not have a mirror handy you should be able to imagine one. If you do not have a reflection, then you do not need a mirror. If you cannot remember how to smile or are an inexperienced smiler, this may be a disadvantage when you start to write.

3. Feel good about yourself and your abilities. Take pride in memorable images, even if they are moon- or birth-related. If your poem extends beyond the end of the page, use a footrest to support it and ensure that there is not undue pressure on your bottom and/or thighs.

4. For comfort and support, adjust your preconceptions and linguistic framework. Believe in your words. They have meaning, but will not find a purpose without you.

5. Avoid limericks.

6. Your own life should be approximately a hand's length away from the edge of the poem. That should leave sufficient room to place several other lives in the space within the poem—at least one, but hopefully more. When imagining your own life or those of others, adjust your viewing distance to suit, but always ensure a slightly unusual viewing angle. As a rough guide, your eyes should be able to focus on the point in the distance where reality is almost but not quite indistinguishable from imagination.

7. Associate with successful poems. Do what they do. When faced with choices, make the choice a successful poem would make. They may support you when you can no longer support yourself.

8. Do not be afraid to use some form of reference material if it supports your posture. You should not have to stretch excessively for a word that is appropriate, apt, apposite, apropos, fitting, felicitous, germane, pertinent, relevant, suitable or to the point. If faced with a choice of words, especially involving any that are more usually employed in lesser activities such as preparing to-do lists, filling in passport applications or texting someone to say when you expect to be home, pick the word which hangs back and refuses to look straight at you. Commit to every word you use.

9. Don't blow all the capital of your inspiration on one epic poem when you could invest it in many smaller poems over a longer period of time.

10. Avoid unsuccessful poems. Do not under any circumstances persevere with negative poems. Negative poems are toxic; they destroy, they do not build. They are vampires that can live only by draining life from other poems. Avoid all whiny poems, complaining poems, poems apportioning blame, poems which suck their thumbs when they should just grow up and, most importantly, poems which tell you what to do.

11. Write what you are best at and what you get the most satisfaction from. Do not bow to the false gods of free verse; good rhyme is not a crime (though the villanelle is the road to Hell).

12. Your body position should be 'squared-up' to the subject matter, but you should avoid all other hard edges and planar surfaces. A good poem is curved. A great poem is several harmoniously-arranged curves, interlinking and yet irregular.

13. Do not be constrained by your initial plan. Sometimes less is more, but there will be times when more is more. If the poem wants to get drunk and argue with you, let it. Sleep with every poem you write, and if it looks as good in the morning as it did when you went to bed with it—it may just be the one you've been looking for.

Brompton Cocktails

I serve the lonely drinker in the corner,
wasted, and yet seeking something stronger.

Their drink of choice was mixed for me
by Registrars, a tried and trusted recipe

passed along in secret. None see the art
of its making, no-one notes it on the chart,

but still the glass is filled. A quarter-gill
of morphine, bitter as the coldest gall,

is thickened by a snowdrift of cocaine,
because the drinker must be lucid. Pain

should now be easing off, the wake
of a departing boat, but should it break

through there are subtle notes of cannabis,
to quell the nausea, its own antagonist.

Add Tanqueray (though any decent brand
will do); a dash of syrup to remind

us that this life might never be as sweet again.
Finally, dilute with water to your taste. Drain

in one, or sip it like a princess, the effect
is just the same; a measure of faith over fact.

It's a quarter to three, the bar is now closed.
Set 'em up, sister. One more for the road.

Rollback

Here are the reverse engineers
to reduce the irreducible,
drive a chisel into the mortar,
unbuild the house to build a wall.
Those who huddle under statues
are dispersed, and in towers
elevators full of women only rise
so far before they fall.

The hand we used to wipe
before we shook, we now wipe
afterwards, or keep in pockets.
We used to party at year's end,
set off rockets kept back
from November; now we
sleep our way to midnight,
houses creaking full of dark.

We cried at things; shattered
cities, babies on the foreshore,
but now the tears roll up
our cheeks, back into eyes,
tired of accommodations
and even the wind blows
the other way. It doesn't matter,
but we remember when it did.

The language is regressing
into gesture, nuance, silence.
When we speak, it's of repeal,
rethink, reverse. We gather
at the well, but every bucket
is more brackish than the last,
and soon we'll have to mix

the hydrogen and oxygen ourselves.
The news blackout holds, but there's
a looping nature documentary;
a curious fish steps backward
off the beach and back into the sea,
feet turning to fins, to waving stumps,
scales flaking away, flesh dissolving
into bacteria, the idea of bacteria,
then back to a time before ideas.

Tiny Clanger Triolet

Here on this moon your world grows dimmer
please let us light it with our song.
We may be small, but see! We shimmer
here on this moon. Your world grows dimmer,
your inner child is getting thinner,
forgetting where it once belonged;
here on this moon. Your world grows dimmer;
please let us light it with our song.

Galaxy

I heard a voice as I was lying in the gutter,
saying that the universe is cold and bitter,
how 85% of it is cocoa solids, little lighter
than the cellar of oblivion, and barely sweeter.

See the stars, it said, how they drift and scatter
in the vacuum, hanging motes of glitter,
a billion nibs of light that soon will stutter,
shatter. This is the darkness of the matter.

I Found This at My Ear

—After W. S. Graham

I found this at my ear when I awoke,
my keeper coming, jangling his keys,
a gentle hum, a breathing-out of smoke.

The clock chimed from the dampness of the hall.
You loitered before padding up the stairs.
In coming to I heard the breakers call.

You came late, though you didn't know the hour
and in your hushed arrival was the dream
of finding me asleep, beyond all power,

yet here I was, alive. My love, you spoke
the beat of insect wings. The shore gulls roared.
I found this at my ear when I awoke.

If You Are Not as Tall as Me
You Cannot Ride This Ride

If you are not as wall as me you cannot build this high
If you are not as well as me you cannot drink this deep
If you are not as will as me you cannot make this leap
If you are not as hill as me you cannot see this far
If you are not as hell as me you cannot feed this fire
If you are not as held as me you cannot raise this arm
If you are not as hold as me you cannot keep this calm
If you are not as cold as me you cannot ice this vein
If you are not as bold as me you cannot horse this rein
If you are not as bond as me you cannot glue this crack
If you are not as band as me you cannot beat this back
If you are not as land as me you cannot root this soil
If you are not as hand as me you cannot bear this toil
If you are not as hang as me you cannot fall this soon
If you are not as sang as me you cannot hold this tune
If you are not as sane as me you cannot be this touched
If you are not as same as me you cannot change this much
If you are not as game as me you cannot play this rhyme
If you are not as tame as me you cannot cage this time
If you are not as tale as me you cannot speak this side
If you are not as tall as me you cannot ride this ride

...Who Loved This Place

...who knew the names of so many plants he forgot his own.
...who woke one morning to find her hair ravelled to bindweed.
...whose smile was like stepping through a hothouse door.
...who brought many friends here, but only in bad weather.
...who came in the autumn but could not be over-wintered.
...who could not decide between the topsoil and the stars.
...who grew nothing in her garden except older.
...who read *Keep Off The Grass*, but could not help herself.
...whose love was one part fertiliser and two parts weedkiller.
...who watered a rose that should have been dead-headed.
...who gave his life for water, light and a space to bloom.
...who was always falling stamen, stalk and pedicel.
...whose middle names were hardy, cordate, everbearing.
...who was born among nettles but perished a succulent.
...who traded the certainty of frost for faith in snowdrops.
...who came here in the wilting dusk and can never now leave.

Just Need to Check You're Not a Robot

—From Isaac Asimov's Three Laws of Robotics

1. *A robot may not injure a human being or, through inaction, allow a human being to come to harm.*
A girl showed affection; I regifted it as hopelessness.
I held the chasubles while priests stoned an agnostic.
I shot a man in Renfrew just to watch him die.
I tested positive but slept around. Love is all is all.

2. *A robot must obey orders given it by human beings except where such orders would conflict with the First Law.*
Staff toilet. Members only. No entry. You're no the boss o me.
I hear what you're saying and I don't like what I'm hearing.
Twenty's plenty. Thirty's dirty. Forty's naughty.
I have two rules. The first is not to reveal too much.

3. *A robot must protect its own existence as long as such protection does not conflict with the First or Second Law.*
My voice rings across a seething pub; want a picture, fuckface?
Golem wrestling. Swimming with kraken. A man needs a hobby.
Wine by the Methuselah, chocolate by the kilo: all things in immoderation.
My named is R Icarus Knievel and I am my own stunt double.

Dementia Song

What should I write now? Should I write?
I still have stories to tell. I remember
when there was more than day/night,
that my birthday fell in   November.

December? Yes, of course. What . day?
Are you sure? Yes, of course it was.
         If I had   knew. Known? What did I say?
Well, this story won't tell itself because

this story. This story   of small deaths
        of bereavements   by decree. Degree?
What did I say? Yes of course. The test
is in the held notes of   the   memory,

my longs not being   what they. Lungs.
   The held   notes of the memory.   Hands
are unlearning me.   I still have songs
         to sing. Small deaths. You understand.

I'm talking but   the words   of course
  I haven't forgotten. Memory is   tracing
         paper, outlines   no detail.   Gets worse
      the more I. What why are we whispering?

You're talking   about me? You were.
         What are you   what are you saying
about me? This story. I know   where
it ends. I don't know,   something

About. Bereament.   Reavement.
                What? Last night?   When?
                    Talking about me. The treatment
  I don't know where it ends.

[66]

      I don't feel well. not well.
 Sing me a song. shall we?
    song to sing.   shall
   we? Yes.   who is she?

I don't know her.
        she's still singing
   all night. I don't know what for
       phone. Phone ringing

Do we have a phone?
    Are we in? you are.
Are you? yes. We're alone
   aren't we. we are.   here.

   are we?
songs to sing.
         [tell me a story]
      something

  [who are you]
       stop.   write
.   ? .
      [.]

Treppenwitz

German: A smart response which occurs to you only after a conversation has ended

—for Avijeet Das

When they asked me for my name
I should have answered *I am the rain.*

When they asked me where I lived
I should have answered *down a grid.*

When they asked for my date of birth
I should have said *April 1st. No, July 4th.*

When they asked me for the specific year
I should have said *I don't know; I wasn't there.*

When they asked the place I was born in
I should have said *somewhere in the morning.*

When they asked my occupation
I should have said *I'm in Industrial Fabrication.*

Had I had any previous convictions?
I should have said *one for aggravated contradiction.*

Why did I think I had been detained?
I should have said *is it the TV licence again?*

Where was I at the time of the incident?
I should have said *golfing with the president.*

When they asked about my associates
I should have said *diplomats and astronauts.*

From whom did I take my orders?
I should have said *only from my mother.*

What was to be my next target?
I should have said *to get a better haircut.*

Would I like to make a signed confession?
I should have said *what was the usual convention?*

When they asked me how do you plead?
I should have said *I find it works best on my knees.*

When they told me I was guilty on all charges
I should have said *I'll hold out for a pardon.*

When they asked if I had any last requests
I should have said *I don't know. What do you suggest?*

Everyman's Encyclopaedia, 1972

—A partwork

A—Bamboccio
Back then, single initials were enough for anyone,
middle names being bourgeois affectations
and not for the likes of us, we simpletons
we rag dolls. Being all things and none,

Bamboo—Cachuca
we did not hide in groves or in the long grass
but in plain sight; in dingy pubs, on shop floors,
sometimes shuffling round department stores,
dancing solo or in pairs with girls from our class.

Cacique—Condottieri
We accepted no leaders; none you'd recognise,
although some courted our votes, our taxes,
waving airily at us, sending up detachments
of hirelings to tell us how it was foolish to be wise.

Conductance—Electron
The current flowed, but only in one direction;
Christmas Club and fifty pence for the meter,
holidays in Anglesey, Pampas Green Vauxhall Viva,
the atomic structure of life, from birth to pension.

Electron Microscope—Ghadames
But look closer; what new processes asserted
themselves beyond the lens, what grew there?
Knowledge; starting small—sand in the air,
precipitating into a pearl in the desert,

Ghana—Inertial Navigation
then spilling across the golden coast of itself,
until it could not be contained by any border
or reckoned by compass. We trusted this water
to be safe to drink, and filled our shelves

Infallibility—Lobachevsky
with books which, because they existed,
could never be wrong, because they spoke
could not be misheard. We built week by week
using a geometry to which we were apprenticed

Lobau—Myxomycetes
from our naked days, doing as we were told,
and yet sensing when it was ok not to do what
we were told, not keeping off the grass, not
throwing away the cheese because of the mold.

Naafi—Pillnitz
It was fine to have no aim, ambition, fuck-all
interest, but some of us knew there was more,
even if we didn't want it. Our own shade of poor
meant we could afford day trips to castles

Pillory—Santa Barbara
without wanting to live in them, posing in stocks
and laughing at how they used to treat the serfs
in darker times, before the softening of the earth.
Once, our mission was clear; life was an empty box,

Santa Catalina—Thomas A Kempis
to be carried till strength ran out, at which time
it would carry us, not to some worker's Avalon
but back to the beginning, an endless imitation
of ourselves. It takes these volumes to define

Thomas Aquinas—Zyryanovsk
our better purpose: to be higher than we are;
to mine every last jewel; to revise and refine;
to avoid the dead ends in the ancient design;
to find the sum of all truths in weekly parts.

Errata
* *The Vauxhall Viva may not have been Pampas Green;*
* *For 'mold' read 'mould' (incorrectly Americanised);*
* *Naafi, as non-standard acronym, should be capitalised;*
* *Finding 'the sum of all truths' is not guaranteed.*

Two Poems for the Undecided

'Indecision may or may not be my problem'. (Jimmy Buffet)

1.

There goes Jock Tamson's bull,
two farmers yanking at the same old chain.
Meanwhile I've been lowing at my stall
to little effect, just as happy in the rain
as in the sun, whether it's milk today, or none.

Maybe I should slip the old ring
from my nose, find out what the rope
is lashed to at the other end,
but it's simpler to accept that hope
is just a sop, and wait for it all to bloody stop.

2.

Give me just a minute, or an hour,
to go through all the papers one more time,
plot the arguments against the normal
distribution curve, find the shoogly line
of least resistance, question every witness.

I seek a middle way, as undemanding
as a mother's kiss, a non-intervention pact
in the event of revolution, an unforked path
that means I do not have to face the fact
that all this noise is the sum of our choice.

So I've joined the Party With No Name,
campaigning on the ticket *think now act later,*
whose manifesto runs to a thousand pages,
each printed on responsibly sourced fly paper.
The truth is double-sided. Yes? No? Undecided.

On Being Mistaken for Another Poet

—for A. B. Jackson

You've seen their name on Facebook, and in real books.
You go to readings but they're never there. No-one knows
them much, but then they don't know you. You look
to engineer encounters in the places where they go, although
it's possible they don't exist in this dimension. You pluck
up courage for an accidental rendezvous. They do not show.

Like an acned youth, you send a scratchy billet-doux
by intermediary to where they work; by return, *there's no-one
here by that name.* What powers keep their secret, who
is tipping them the wink? If they were ever there, they're gone.
You picture them aflame with drink, laughing with their crew
at all your ploys. Their latest book arrives from Amazon:
in sour light, the scowling photo on the flyleaf could be you,
and who at your age doesn't seek a flattering diffusion of the sun?

One look inside its pages sparks the matchhead of your fears;
a rich and sweet compendium of poems of an elegant design.
The tone and form intricate, unfamiliar, yet the voice is clear,
unequivocal, the narrative a mirror of your own, but realigned.
A hand has reached inside the crevice of your mind, filched ideas
you thought were yours alone, and all those ornate lines
about the sea, the dawn, are gone. What remain are souvenirs
of your recession, all your notebooks emptying, your soul blind.

Years pass. You've been absorbed; your words blown like sand
while those they stole form monuments. Could you be dead?
It's possible that words were all you were. Now you stand,
a spectre by a roaring pyre of manuscripts, unread,
unreadable. Mobile rings, a voice familiar: *Hello my friend.
I am the poet you may yet become. Better get a pen.*

Succession Planning

—*for Marjorie Lotfi*

Bepishvaz-e-janeshin   بپیشواز جانشین

Because a new sun must rise tomorrow
The old one will need a place to rest.

تا که افتابی نو بدرخشد فردا
خورشید باید در جایی بسر ارد امشب

Ta keh aftabi no bederakhshad farda
Khorshid bayad dar jayee besar arad emshab

Because a visitor may arrive tomorrow
The house must be ready today.

تاکه مهمانی شاید ز در رسد فردا
کلبه را باید اماده ساخت امروز

Ta keh mehmani shayd ze dar resad farda
Kolbeh ra bayad amadeh sakht emrooz

Because we cook with saffron tomorrow
We must water the crocuses today.

تا که خوراک معطر باشد فردا
مزرعه زعفران را باید ابیاری کرد امروز

Ta keh khorak mo'attar bashad farda
Mazraeye za'fran ra bayad abyari kard emrooz

Because others will need poems tomorrow
Someone must write them today.

تا که دیگران شعر خوانی کنند فردا
شاعران باید شعر سرایی کنند امروز

Ta keh digharan she'r khani konand farda
Sha'eran bayad she'r saraaee konand emrooz

[75]

Enquiry Desk, Scottish Poetry Library

Do you have the one
with that poem they read at the funeral
in that movie?

Do you have the one
with that poem that they used to make us
learn at secondary school?

Do you have the one
with that poem that the Librarians decided was
too beautiful to catalogue and classify?

Do you have the one
with that poem that knows the difference between
ae thing and *anither thing*?

Do you have the one
with that poem that sat in the corner for ten years and then
exploded like a grenade in a crowded space?

Do you have the one
with that poem from the box of love letters
the city keeps under its bed?

Do you have the one
with that poem that identifies the chemical properties
of the ghosts of ideas it contains?

Do you have the one
with that poem that is a cache of weapons
which can never be put beyond use?

Do you have the one
with that poem that has learned to impersonate
other poems it has never met?

Do you have the one
with that poem that has mastered chiaroscuro
yet can also emulsion a room in an hour?

Do you have the one
with that poem that stole into my lover's bed
when I wasn't reading it?

Do you have the one
with that poem that is bigger on the inside
than on the outside?

Do you have the one
—you must have it—
with that poem that is a Library in itself,
each leaf a life we might one day live?

I don't know what it's called
but it calls, it calls.

Acknowledgments

Some of the poems in this collection have appeared in magazines and other publications, including *The Darg, Dead Guid Scots, Dostoyevsky Wannabe, Dundee University Review of the Arts, Federation of Writers Scotland anthology, Firth, New Boots and Pantisocracies, Our Botanic Garden, Poetry Scotland, The Poets' Republic, Scotia Extremis, The Umbrellas of Edinburgh, The View From Olympia*. Thanks to the editors of those publications for allowing me to use those poems.

'Galaxy' appeared in Helena Nelson's *Wrapper Rhymes* project. 'Gongoozlers' was selected by Jo Bell for her *Canal Poems*. 'Dementia Song' was commended in the 2021 Hippocrates Poetry Prize.

Sincere thanks go to members of the Soutar Writers and Dundee Poetry Workshop. Particular thanks go to Sheila Wakefield, Founder and Editor at Red Squirrel Press, Elizabeth Rimmer, my editor on this collection, and Gerry Cambridge for design and typesetting.

A NOTE ON THE TYPES

The poems in this book are set in
Dante, which in its metal form, designed by
Giovanni Mardersteig and released in 1957, was called
'one of the great achievements of twentieth-century
typography' by no less than Robert Bringhurst. It is a beautiful
text face which was released in digital form in 1993.

The titles are in Avenir, a sans serif
designed by Adrian Frutiger and released in
its original version in 1988.